By: Robert W. Rushing, Jr.

William Wilberforce Press

2014

So many people have described the experience to me. Much of the description, though, is always the same. "It took just a second, but remembering it now, it seems like it took a long time." For some reason, the mind seems to record a traumatic event like an automobile accident in slow motion. Small details stick in the mind, many seemingly insignificant.

Likewise, most people have the same thoughts immediately afterwards. These are invariably towards the safety of themselves, their passengers, and possibly the other driver. If they are fortunate enough not to be seriously injured, they are nevertheless probably shocked and disoriented.

I have been in one serious automobile accident myself. It was on a winding road headed towards the coast in a hard driving rain. I was alone. Moments after the collision, I remember looking myself over, and thinking that I was lucky. The car appeared to be totaled, but I saw no scratch on myself. Moments later I looked down and noticed that my white button down shirt was turning red.

By that time, I had already been involved in countless other accident cases, as an attorney. Despite that experience, standing there in the driving rain, bleeding, I did relatively little of what I will advise you to do in this book.

I was fortunate in that my injuries turned out to be on the lighter side. There were a few stitches, and some deep bruises that more or less took care of themselves. The car was a total loss, but that claim was taken care of relatively quickly, as is the norm.

However, I still have one permanent scar. It is also a permanent reminder of just how close I came to disaster. It starts just beneath my left ear, a few inches from the corroded artery. This was the source of the blood on my shirt. I had come within inches of a lethal wound.

I was very lucky. For some people, the most serious injury is internal, hidden from view and possibly from diagnosis. It lingers like a ticking time bomb, prepared to do its worst hours, days, or even months later.

This is why I advise anyone who is in an automobile accident, no matter how minor or harmless it might seem at the time, to get medical care. Far too many people have suffered serious consequences or even died because they refused medical care at the scene, then went about their business unaware of internal bleeding or organ damage.

When you are in an automobile accident, you want closure. From a psychological standpoint, most of us want to move on from what is, at best, a nuisance and at worst, a difficult and traumatic experience. If there is money coming, the sooner we get it the better. Besides, few of us want the disruption of repeated visits to see health care providers, insurance adjusters, and even lawyers.

Besides that, there are generally lots of outside sources pressing you to resolve the situation quickly. If you have dependents, the temptation is to settle your case in a hurry to take care of them, especially if ability to work is in doubt. If your claim has value, the insurance company will do everything possible to get you to settle the case quickly, for less than it is worth, before you receive any bad medical news.

The health care providers might be looking to your claim for payment. If you are able to work, your employer is unlikely to have much patience with any disruption caused by your situation. All of these factors, and possibly more, will build up like pressure behind a cork, to make you settle your claim early.

However, this is not always in your best interest. While marriage may not be forever, a signed and witnessed signature on a release is. Once you have settled your claim, whatever happens after the fact is your problem. No attorney enjoys telling a desperate potential client that nothing can be done to help them, because they settled their case too cheap and too soon.

What is needed is a level headed decision based on the facts, made only after the facts are available. Anything less is a roll of the dice that that could have life changing implications if something goes wrong.

This book will show you how to gather and document the facts, and then make the right decisions. It will help you understand the other players in the process, their motives and agendas, and help you decide who if anyone, to trust. It will keep you from making the big, irrevocable mistakes which can cripple or destroy your claim from the beginning. Whether your claim is settled, or ultimately tried before a jury, the idea is to put you in the best possible position in a situation where nothing, and no one, is what they appear to be.

CHAPTER ONE: AT THE SCENE

First, let me acknowledge reality. Chances are that you are reading this well after the fact of your accident. This means that the opportunity to document physical evidence at the scene of your accident has most likely passed, for better or worse.

Still, it is worthwhile to address the issue. However much time has passed, there are still things that can be done to document what and how things happened, and thereby strengthen your case. Ideally, these things would be done as soon as possible, but better late than never. There is still plenty of evidence to be found in a cold case, as anyone who watches even a little TV is aware.

Immediately after an accident, there are obvious issues of concern. We have already discussed the first and most obvious of these, the safety of yourself and everyone else involved. However, "safety" is a term which can involve more than just the possibility of physical injury. It is worth pointing out that in some areas, criminals have been known to intentionally hit a vehicle to force a stop, so that they can do harm to the occupants. There is also the issue of road rage.

This raises the question of whether you can trust the occupants of the other car. When in doubt, remain inside your locked vehicle. While fleeing the scene is not an option except in the most extreme cases, there is no reason to risk your safety by approaching a stranger if you do not feel comfortable in doing so. Instead, call for help immediately and wait.

In the meantime, make a note of the license tag of the other vehicle if this is possible. You cannot be sure that the other driver will not attempt to leave, particularly if he or she is clearly at fault. Make the best possible notes as to the color, year, make and model of the vehicle.

While you wait, it is also a good idea to call a friend or family member and make them aware of the situation. You might need their help and the sooner they arrive the better.

At this point, I would mention that for obvious reasons, this advice is made with the assumption that there are no serious life threatening injuries. You would obviously do everything possible to attend to anyone at the scene in such a situation, and that concern would supersede any other. If an ambulance arrives first, answer their questions thoroughly and carefully.

Keep in mind, however, that these people will be taking and keeping notes. While the medical personnel are not there to investigate the accident, assign fault, and enforce the law, whatever you say about the circumstances of the accident are relevant to their work. For that reason, your statements at the scene will show up in the medical records.

No matter what you may think at the time, NEVER admit to being at fault at the scene of the accident. While the instinct to do so is admirable, there are two serious problems here. The first involves the limited nature of your perception of the event.

Have you ever heard the children's story about the blind men who touched different parts of an elephant? One touched the trunk, and thought the elephant was much like a snake. The second touched the leg, and though the elephant was like a tree with a huge trunk, etc. My point is that there is a great deal you do not know at this point, as you have only seen a small part of what happened. This is no time to jump to conclusions.

The second important reason is anyone who hears that you admitted at the scene to causing the accident will believe you. This will be true no matter what you may find out later to the contrary.

If you have time before law enforcement arrives, spend it thinking through the circumstances of the accident. While you do not want to lie, you also do not want to incriminate yourself and cause criminal and civil liability. If you have passengers, ask them what they saw and heard. Take a look around and check out the environment for physical evidence as to what has happened.

Since practically everyone has a camera on their phone these days, take pictures of everything. The most important things to document at the scene are the following:

1. The resting places of the two vehicles in the accident.
2. The area of impact on each vehicle.
3. All physical damage to the outside of each vehicle.
4. Any skid marks on the road.
5. Any damage to other objects in proximity to the accident.
6. Any debris from the vehicles on the highway or elsewhere.
7. Damage to the interior of your car.
8. Physical injuries to yourself and other passengers.

When the officer arrives, approach him immediately. Whatever he or the other driver says or does, maintain a calm and civil manner. The worst mistake you can make at this point is to alienate the investigating officer by having him or her peg you as a hothead who is likely at fault.

Most likely, the other driver will be face to face with you. Begin by asking about his or her health. This can be difficult to do under the circumstances, especially if this person is less than pleasant. However, I can document clients of mine who have kept their cool and been amazingly polite under far worse circumstances.

For example, I once represented an Englishman who had served in the navy. He had a hobby of building operating scale replicas of ships. This involved more than just gluing together a few parts and painting them. Each build would be a project that extended over a period of years. When the model was finished, it had lights, a working motor, a rudder, and sometimes even cannon. It could be operated in the water from a remote control.

Right before his accident, from what he told me, he was watching the Tonight Show. No. He didn't have a television in his SUV. Actually, he was in his living room.

What happened was that a neighbor was returning home from the graveyard shift at work. It was very late, and he was exhausted. He simply fell asleep at the wheel, swerved off the road, and drove through my client's living room.

By incredible luck, his pregnant wife had just exited the room, headed for the bedroom at the other end of the house. He had just stood up from his chair to follow her. Nobody was hurt, but the room was where he housed his collection of ships, all of which were destroyed.

As the driver forced his door open, causing more bricks to come loose from the wall, he said "Always good to have company, but next time, could you consider using the door?"

If you're too angry to find relief that the situation was not worse, or humor in the circumstances, remember this. Everything you say at that moment is likely to be repeated to a jury, should your case ever come to trial. I once tried a case in which the defendant said that the first thing my client said to him after the accident was "You just destroyed a seventy five thousand dollar vehicle!"

You can imagine how that went over in small, rural county in which nobody on the jury panel had ever even thought of owning a car that expensive. The Defendant was clearly at fault in the case, but I had to spend most of my time from that point onward convincing the jury that my client was not a rich jerk. The offhand comment might have costs him thousands of dollars.

So, is it important to have the first word? That depends. If the other driver looks humbled and apologetic, and appears ready to explain how he or she caused the wreck, let him have the floor.

On the other hand, if he or she is about to tell a tall tale make the officer aware that you are not in agreement with his version of the facts. This does not mean that you have to cut him or her off, nodding your head, or a few cursory "no's" will suffice. You will get your turn to speak.

If there are witnesses, the officer will most likely speak to them. It is always a good idea to attempt to find out if these people have any sort of relationship with the other driver. In the case of a passenger, it will be obvious.

However, in our age of fast and easy communication, it is possible that the driver has arranged for someone to travel to the scene. I have seen cases in which this person would claim to be a witness. Keep this in mind if the witness seems to linger in proximity to the other driver, or to have an unusually comfortably rapport with him or her.

As to any and all witnesses at the scene, you should do the following:

1. Get the name, address, telephone number, and e mail address of the witnesses if they are willing to provide same;
2. If possible, get a summary of what would testify to;
3. Try to get relevant details as to circumstances, such as how far away they were at the time of the accident, how clear their view was, whether they were distracted, etc.
4. Make notes as to your impressions of the person. This would include things like a physical description, notes about demeanor (was she concerned about the people involved? Annoyed by the disruption? Does she seem likely to be willing to get involved later?)

Do your best to get information, but do not be pushy. The last thing you want to do at this point is make an enemy.

In all probability, somebody is going to get a ticket. If it seems like you are going to be that person, explain your side of things to the officer, but do not argue. If there are witnesses at the scene who can help you, urge the officer to talk to them.

As a general rule, when he or she reaches for the ticket book, the deal is done. Do not refuse to sign the ticket. Signing it is not an admission of guilt. It is only a promise to appear in court at the designated time and place. While it is beyond the scope of this book, the companion book in this series "The Speed Trap Bible" is a detailed discussion of how and when to contest a traffic ticket.

Do not refuse medical care, unless you are absolutely certain that you were not hurt. Otherwise, out of an abundance of caution, it is worth the time and expense to be examined in the emergency room.

If this is impossible, make an appointment as soon as possible with your regular doctor. Keep in mind that if you fail to get treatment, the insurance company will beat you over the head with this fact later. The argument will be that, if you had really been hurt, you would have treated at the time. For many reasons, this is a highly questionable assumption. Still, most people believe it.

Is it necessary to call for an ambulance? Not if you have another way to get to the hospital. This is a question that can be answered through common sense. The principle benefit of the ambulance is speed. If your situation requires one, you will most likely be in no position to refuse. Otherwise, consider alternatives.

CHAPTER TWO: THE PLAYERS AND THE GAME

At this point, you will be making some choices. They come quickly in the days following an accident, and many are irrevocable. You will be forced to deal with a cast of characters who may or may not have your best interests at heart, and may or may not be trustworthy.

While I cannot evaluate the individuals you will be dealing with, I can go a long way towards helping you to do so. This can be done by explaining their jobs, and by extension, their agendas.

Player Number 1: The Insurance Adjuster: Actually, you will almost certainly deal with more than one insurance adjuster. For openers, if you own the vehicle, there will be a property adjuster or two. If liability in your case is in dispute, there might be one or several more of these on the other side of the case.

Often, personal injury claims are handled today by a "team" of adjusters. There is rapid turnover among the teams, and also in the companies generally. The truth is, what individual actually handles your claim is far less important than it was ten years ago.

This is because of the fact that the decision making authority of adjusters has been severely limited, as the carriers rely increasingly on computer programs such as Allstate's "Colossus" to produce an upper and lower range of settlement authority. It is difficult or impossible for an adjuster to exceed the range of authority dictated by the computer software, even if he or she is convinced that this should be done.

In general, here is what you need to know about insurance adjusters. The job of an insurance adjuster is not unlike that of someone operating a pawn shop. His job is to resolve your claim for his company.

Company, as cheaply as possible and ideally for nothing.

It is important to understand the difference in marketing and reality. Insurance companies are not the community oriented, folksy operations they portray themselves as on TV. Rather, they are multinational corporations richer than most countries. Their adjusters are evaluated, promoted, and awarded bonuses based upon performance; in other words, how good they are at not handing out the company money.

If you've watched the show "Pawn Stars" you have seen the fantasy version of claim negotiation. The analogy might not be precise, but the process involves buying and selling, and a certain interpretation of ethics.

On "Pawn Stars" a customer walks off the street with something which may or may not be highly valuable. Much like an insurance adjuster, the clerk on "Pawn Stars" has the job of setting a value and purchasing the item. On the show, it is some kind of tangible object. In your case, the item of value is your injury or property claim. Otherwise, the situation is the same.

Here's where the fantasy part comes in. Invariably, the "Pawn Stars" guy says something to the effect of "this thing might be worth a lot of money and I want to be fair to you. Let's call in expert and get an appraisal."

While I love the show, this is not how life works. In real life, if the owner of the pawn shop thinks your item is valuable, he will do everything in his power to get it out of your hands as cheaply as possible. His profits and survival are not based on brokering a fair deal with you. They are based on buying low and selling high.

Likewise, the insurance adjuster cannot, by definition, worry too much about the fairness of your situation. He is being evaluated based upon performance. Paying you a little (or a lot) less can get him his raise, promotion, or trip to Hawaii.

Like most other professionals, he is trained to do his job well. He attends seminars and job training intended to teach him how to communicate with an accident victim, gain their trust and take advantage. There is an old saying, "Keep your friends close and your enemies even closer." The adjuster is trained to work on this principle.

This does not mean that he or she is a bad person, just doing a job.

PLAYER NUMBER 2: THE LAWYER.

Before we tackle the big question of "Do I need one?" let's first discuss the role of the attorney. First the good news, unlike the adjuster, the lawyer you hire is legally and ethically bound to advance your best interests. His success or failure is evaluated based on how well things work out for you, not the other way around.

However, this is not the whole picture. It might be that for some reason, your situation makes an attorney an unnecessary expense. For example, you might have medical bills in excess of the maximum insurance coverage available from the at-fault driver, and his or her insurance company admitting liability. (Importantly, there could be additional insurance coverage available, in which case the services of a lawyer might be crucial.)

If this is the case, there would be little or nothing for the attorney to do but order the check, lop off one third of the proceeds for himself, and hand over the rest. This would be especially true in no fault states, in which the accident victim will be dealing with his or her own insurance company.

This might also be true where the damages in the case are too small to justify the expense of an attorney. For example, if you received treatment in the emergency room, and nothing more, you might wish to simply negotiate a settlement with the carrier which will cover the expense and hopefully a bit more for pain and suffering. (Keep in mind that you should err on the side of caution when it comes to treatment. The longer you delay in seeing a doctor, the less likely an insurance company is to concede that your problem is related to the accident.)

Also, the lawyer himself is subject to conflicting priorities. Look for signs that your attorney is overburdened. If you have friends who have cases pending with the firm, ask them if things are going well. Are their telephone calls being returned promptly? Are they being advised of the status of their case? When you are in the office, take a look around. Are files and papers stacked everywhere? Do the employees seem to be stressed out and in crisis mode?

If this is the case, beware. This lawyer is unlikely to do a lot of preparation before your court date, as he or she will be too busy putting out fires. Also, chances are that the claim will be resolved slowly, unless it has great value relative to his other pending cases.

A less apparent conflicting interest is the financial situation of the lawyer. If the lawyer is in debt, or anticipates a major personal or professional expense, watch out. This might cause him or her to pressure you to settle your claim, whether or not it is in your long term best interest.

The bottom line is this. The attorney by definition has the job of advancing your interests, unlike the insurance adjuster. However, this does not necessarily mean that you need an attorney, or a particular attorney.

PLAYER NUMBER THREE: THE HEALTH CARE PROVIDER.

Few people understand the power that a doctor has over a personal injury claim. In some ways, it is far greater than that of the lawyer. The doctor does the following:

1. Your general practitioner or emergency room physician will refer you to any necessary specialist, or not.
2. Your treating physician will make the initial evaluation and describe your injuries and symptoms. Those medical records will be seen as the definitive source of this information to insurance adjusters and juries.
3. Your treating physician will resolve the issue of whether or not you have any permanent injuries and

the extent of same. This will be one of the most important bases by which the value of your claim will be determined.
4. Your treating physician will determine whether you should be out of work, and when you should return to work.
5. Your treating physician will determine whether you should have surgery, and be essential in arrange all of the particulars of same.
6. Your treating physician will determine when your medical care should end.

As such, it is essential that your doctor cares about your claim, or at least is not hostile to your claim. It is not safe to assume either. Many doctors detest working with attorneys, seeing any request to assist with the case as an intrusion upon their time.

When this is the case, the result can be a stand-off between you, the doctor, and your lawyer. Unfortunately, it is a conflict you cannot walk away from, as his records are the key to your claim.

Then there are the other kind of treating physicians. Some clinics and practitioners actively court and cater to the personal injury trade. Frequently but not always, these individuals are in the field of alternative health care, in fields such as pain management or chiropractic. Opinions differ as to their effectiveness, and in court they are invariably attacked as "ambulance chasers" and the like.

On the positive side, they tend to have a lot of familiarity with the soft tissue injuries which result from low impact automobile accidents. Consequentially, they can be effective. They also tend to be much more user friendly, for example, being willing to wait for payment until the claim is resolved.

If you are represented by a lawyer, he or she might have a working relationship with a physician or clinic of this sort. Be aware that if your case goes to trial, the doctor is likely to be asked how many referrals he or she has received from your lawyer, and about their working arrangement.

CHAPTER THREE: THE PROPERTY CLAIM/THE HEALING PROCESS

In most cases, you will be contacted quickly by the insurance company. There will be many reasons for this. All of them are related to the best interests of the insurance company, although this will not be apparent.

In all probability, your conversation will be recorded. If you are listening, you will hear the adjuster explain this, or it will be on the recording that plays while you are on hold. Everything you say will be documented, in case it is useful to the insurance carrier. You, on the other hand, will find it difficult or impossible to obtain a copy of the tape later.

You will be asked about your health. This is not out of human concern, but because it is part of the script and necessary to protect the interest of the insurance company. A polite "I'm fine" or "I'm OK" will not be taken as a polite response, but as an adverse admission. Do not say you are fine if you are not fine.

The first conversations should quickly go to the topic of property damage. Here are the important things to know about this part of your claim:

1. The property adjuster will ask for permission to move the vehicle if it has been towed. This is something you

should agree to. The lot is charging by the day to store your car, and in the end, this expense comes out of your settlement. However, before this happens, you should have already taken pictures and video of the damage to the vehicle, and any other evidence it contains. You should also have removed all of your personal property from the vehicle, as it will be impossible to recover it later on.

2. Many adjusters will fail to mention this, but you are entitled to damages for "Loss of Use" of your vehicle if you have not been given a rental car. This amount is generally determined by the cost of a rental comparable to the car you drive. In most states, you will be awarded the daily cost of the rental vehicle until you have been made an offer of settlement for your vehicle or the damages claim.

3. The actual value of your car is based on several factors. Before you negotiate, ask whether the policy awards "replacement cost" of the vehicle. This would be the best case scenario for you. Alternately, consult sources such as Kelly's Blue Book to get reliable values for similar vehicles in your region of the country. The value is based on several factors, including make, model, mileage, options, and condition.

Understand that you are unlikely to come out ahead when your vehicle is totaled. The insurance company is only required to pay you the value of the vehicle, which is often less than the payoff on the loan.

In such cases, the bank will generally receive the check, apply it to your loan, and authorize you to borrow additionally to purchase another car. In such cases, you will want to discuss the issue with your bank prior to signing the check over. Once you have done so, you have lost all leverage. In cases in which the bank has been unwilling to work with my client, I have often advised the bank that I was likewise unwilling to work with them. The property settlement check would go into my file until attitudes changed. Few of my clients could afford to pay for a vehicle that had been destroyed and still make ends meet, so usually the bank would come around to a more mutually advantageous position.

The insurance adjuster will quickly make you an offer on the vehicle, but possibly not a good one. In general, the less the vehicle is worth, the better the chance that you get full value. Expect to be offered what is referred to in the Kelly's Blue Book as "Trade In" value, in other words, what you would be given at a dealership in trade.

Use "retail" or "wholesale" as your target values. You might argue low mileage, options on the vehicle, or excellent condition as factors that should raise the price. Never accept the first offer of settlement without arguing for more. There is always at least some additional money that can be paid in the discretion of the adjuster.

If you have a rental vehicle, there are certain things you should do now. Know that you will not have the car for long, and go ahead and arrange alternative transportation. If you can afford to, go ahead and buy a car, even one that is not one that you want to keep in the long run. You should be able to resell used car later, possibly for a price near to what you paid. This makes more sense than continuing to add up expenses on a rental.

You might also receive a call from another adjuster, the one handling the personal injury part of your claim. Between the two, you should be able to tell how well your claim is going. Here are the signs:

1. If the insurance company that represents the other has made an offer to pay for your vehicle, or the damage to your vehicle. This is a good sign.
2. If instead, they are requesting to take a recorded statement; bad sign.
3. If they are asking you to sign a medical authorization; good sign (but don't do it.)
4. If nobody calls you, very bad sign.

If your car is going to be repaired, choose your own shop. The insurance company will have a list of authorized shops.

Ask for a copy of the list. You should choose a familiar local body shop with a good reputation, ask around, or search the internet for customer feedback. I generally suspect that the shop with first choice status on the list has a bit too cozy of a relationship with the insurance company. This could motivate them to cut corners to benefit he who butters their bread, to your detriment.

If you are asked to give a recorded statement, refuse. You will not be given the opportunity to interview the at fault driver in the same fashion. Why should you subject yourself to the a barrage of questions from a trained professional, intended to lure you into the big mistake which will throw away your case, or slash the value. While the adjuster will tell you otherwise, the statement is not intended to clear things up so that you can be paid. He or she is not authorized to, and will not, take your word on anything where there is evidence to the contrary.

If you are asked to make such a statement, this is a time to consider hiring a lawyer. There is a strong probability that the insurance company has information, accurate or not, that leads it to believe that it can successfully deny the claim. This might come from the accident report, the other driver, or some other source.

If you still want to provide a statement, offer to send a written one. This will avoid the inherent dangers of a spur of the moment interview, and allow you to think out and document what you say.

In the meantime, if you are continuing to treat for your injuries, there are ways to make your future life easier. One of the most important is to collect and keep copies of your bills and medical records as you go along. Most health care providers will charge to provide these at a later date, and the cost is surprisingly high. There will also usually be a fairly long waiting period before you get the records and bills.

The insurance company handling the claim will helpfully offer to gather all of your records, saving you the trouble. The problem with this is that they will want to gather ALL of your records. If the case has significant value, they will dig through your medical history looking for anything that is of help to them.

Mostly, this would be proof of any prior injury or medical condition you might have. It might be possible to claim that this prior injury or condition is the source of your current medical problem, as opposed to the accident. This would keep them from having to pay.

While you are treating, make your appointments reliably. Your records will be scrutinized, and it you are frequently missing, it will be argued that you must not need the treatment. Understand that if you go to trial, the insurance company and its attorneys will use a standard playbook, attempting to portray you as an opportunist looking to make a buck.

You should not even consider settling the personal injury claim until you have been released from medical care. In fact, I would go further. You should not consider settlement until you have been released, and are personally satisfied that you are fully healed and recovered.

After all, you only have one body. I have never, and will never, ask a client to decide what and how much medical treatment to get based upon anything but health factors. The money you receive from your claim, however much it is, will be gone someday. Permanent aches, pains, and physical limitations will stay with you for the rest of your life.

CHAPTER FOUR: NEGOTIATING THE PERSONAL INJURY CLAIM

At some point, your health care provider will release you from care. This is the point at which can begin to look at potentially settling your claim. To do so, you will need all of the following:

1. Complete bills from every health care provider who has treated you as a result of the accident. The totals should be confirmed immediately prior to attempting to settle the case. Hospitals and medical offices are notorious for adding to the balance of a bill long after the final treatment.
2. Complete medical records for the same health care providers. If possible, it is beneficial to get a letter from the treating physician or at least a

discharge summary, detailing the medical problems you have as a result of the accident. Whether or not this is possible will depend on the attitude of the doctor.

3. The accident report from the incident. This will contain the "official" version of what happened to you, and will probably include a determination of fault. The insurance company, and later a jury, will rely heavily on this report. However, it is not admissible in evidence at a trial in most states.

4. The driving record for the other driver involved in your accident. It is necessary that you know the history of the other person involved. For example, if the other driver has a long history of alcohol related offenses, this would raise the value of the claim. Like you, the insurance company would know that this person would get little sympathy from a jury at trial.

5. Any photographs which document injury to yourself or your property. When it comes to explaining physical pain and discomfort, images are better than words.

6. The claim information necessary to get this material to the proper person inside of the insurance company. At a minimum, you will need the following:

   a. The claim number: which can be found on any correspondence sent by the insurance carrier over to you.
   b. The date of incident
   c. The full name of the person insured by the carrier for the at fault driver. (This might or

might not be the other driver. The car might have been loaned, or be titled in the name of a spouse or a business. If this is the case, there is the possibility of filing suit against the third party who owns the vehicle. The legal theory is "negligent entrustment." The point being that under some circumstances, it is careless and irresponsible to hand a person the keys to your car. For example, if they have an unusually bad driving record or a history of substance abuse.)

d. The name of the adjuster handling the claim, and if applicable, the access number for the adjuster. This will also be found on correspondence sent by the insurance company to you.

There is a considerable amount of work to putting all of this together. You do not want to have to do this again, so make copies of everything. If you have a scanner, take the entire package and make a file in your computer.

You will need these documents for several reasons during the negotiation process, and certainly at trial if necessary. You will also need these documents if, as is often the case, the insurance company either loses the package or claims to have lost the package.

There is additional information which can be helpful in the negotiation process. Most importantly, you want to know the insurance limits for the at fault driver. You also want to know whether any other vehicle involved, including your own, has insurance which might cover your damages.

There is no requirement that an insurance adjuster tell you how much coverage is available to satisfy your claim. Most will refuse to do so, unless the policy is for the minimum amount under state law. However, you must ask. It is hard to judge the fairness of any offer without knowing how much money is at least theoretically available.

Also, keep in mind that if you end up filing suit, you will get the answer to this question. The insurance adjuster is already well aware of this.

Your own insurance policy might pay for damages beyond what is covered by the at fault driver, if you have certain types of coverage. The two most common are "uninsured motorist" coverage and "underinsured motorist" coverage. The first covers the situation in which the at-fault driver has no insurance. The second covers the situation in which he or she has insurance, just not enough.

Insurance companies hate to pay underinsured motorist policy claims with a passion. The law in this area is fairly complicated, and varies considerably from state to state. It is important to understand that in most states, if you sign a release in exchange for the insurance proceeds, your right to seek more money from your own insurance company is gone.

Instead, you would agree to release your right to collect against the personal property of the at fault driver. This is often called a "covenant not to execute". The agreement serves the purpose of protecting the at fault driver, as his insurance company is required to do, while also preserving your right to pursue compensation from other insurance policies.

Usually, the amount of the available insurance coverage from all policies is the upper limit on what you can expect to recover. It is possible to go to court and get a verdict for more, but you would have to collect from the personal property of the at fault driver. The law protects certain things from being taken to satisfy a judgment, such as a home and one vehicle. Besides this, it is relatively simple to hide conceal or transfer assets to prevent them from being seized. More to the point, most people do not have much in the way of property that could be taken for this purpose.

So what is your claim worth? Unfortunately, it is impossible to say without information about your particular case. There is no set formula that can tell you what an injured person is entitled to. Insurance companies have attempted to create one, by taking cases with similar circumstances and averaging the verdicts in an area. However, this is not a fair method, and at any rate, is intended to help them calculate <u>exposure</u> as opposed to a reasonable value based upon human experience.

If your medical expenses are substantial, and your condition serious, there might be no problem in figuring what to ask for. Simply send copies of the bills and medical records describing the nature and extent of your injury, and demand all of the insurance coverage. Before you sign anything, check to be sure of what, if any, other insurance coverage exits that might also apply to your claim. If there is such coverage, be sure that you sign nothing that would waive your right to pursue other compensation.

If this is not the case, there used to be a general rule of thumb in less serious accident cases. The going rate was three times the total amount of the "specials", in other words, the actual out of pocket damages. "Specials" would include all medical bills, lost wages, and other out of pocket expenses such as medication. The idea was the one third of the compensation would cover the expenses, one third pain and suffering, and the final third expenses of the claim such as legal fees.

The insurance industry severely reduced payment on claims over the past decade, with Allstate blazing the trail in this direction. In fact, for some time, many personal injury attorneys operated on an automatic "sue" status where Allstate was the insurance carrier, knowing there was little or no chance of a settlement. That situation has moderated somewhat over time, but has not reverted completely back to where it once was.

Nevertheless, if you have no permanent injuries and limited medical treatment as a result of your accident, a settlement in this range would be a good result.

Beyond that, it is at least possible to point out the <u>factors</u> which would be considered in evaluating a claim. Some of these are obvious, but many are not. They include the following:

A. Medical Expenses: These will be considered whether you paid them yourself, or they were paid by a third party provider such as the government or a health care insurer. You will need to collect all medical bills related to your treatment, whether paid or not, and regardless of whom pays them. Also, be aware that a third party provider who pays medical expenses related to an injury claim may seek subrogation benefits. In other words, since there is someone else to pay the bill, they will ask for and be entitled to get their money back.

B. Prescriptions: whatever you spend on medication in or out of a hospital, if related to your injuries, should be calculated into your out of pocket expenses.

C. Being exposes to strong and potent medications: This is the language used in pleading for many years. What it means is that you have suffered the discomfort, physical limitations and other inconveniences related to the use of prescription drugs.

D. Pain and Suffering: This is often the most important factor in a damages claim. One of the better jury arguments I ever heard was, "How much money would you want to be paid every day to have a toothache?" The defense attorney shot up like a rocket and objected, a clear sign that those words cut his case like a knife.

E. Loss of Enjoyment of Life: This involves missing out on all of the things you would otherwise enjoy doing in your life, covering the category beyond work.

F. Loss of Companionship/Consortium: This is a claim that can be brought on behalf of a husband or wife when the spouse has been injured. It can cover things including but not limited to sexual intimacy, lost wages, housekeeping, yard work, walking the dog, or anything else the spouse has to do or do without because of the accident.

G. Lost Wages: Provided that your doctor backs you up on this, you are entitled to be compensated for time out of work due to your injuries.

H. Permanent Disability: This would involve any permanency of your injuries as confirmed by a doctor, including such things as loss of range of motion, scarring and disfigurement, etc.

I. Infliction of Emotional Distress: Not all states permit recovery for this. Of those that permit it, many limit it to intentional acts, or reserve the right for particularly harsh circumstances. For example, some states would allow a mother to sue under this theory who has witnessed a fatal collision involving her child.

J. Punitive Damages: Punitive damages are awarded to punish a defendant for particularly bad acts. The idea being that, if a jury wishes to send a message and discourage bad conduct, it can do so by punishing a wrongdoer with a particularly harsh verdict. The insurance industry has made major headway in limiting the right to pursue and recover punitive damages in many states.

K. Loss of Educational Opportunity: This is sometimes included in pleadings as a separate right to recovery. If you are involved in an educational program, and have paid tuition and begun studies, you should be compensated if your investment of money and time has been lost due to an accident.

This is a fairly comprehensive list, but by no means complete. If you have lost something of value that doesn't seem to fit in a category, bring it into the discussion. You have nothing to lose by trying.

The actual negotiating process works as you might expect. If you have ever haggled over a used car, this is the same with additional formality. The adjuster will begin standard pitch, hoping you are unaware that it is a standard pitch.

You will hear that you had some "contributing" fault to causing the accident, which entitles the carrier to a reduction in the claim. You might hear that you were primarily at fault, even if the accident report and other physical evidence indicate otherwise. You will be told that your doctors charged excessively, whether or not that is the truth.

The important thing is to realize that you are not getting an unbiased, objective opinion about the claim. Rather, you are on the line with a mouthpiece for the insurance company, who has a job to do. On this day, that job involves saving the company money by keeping it away from you. Once you are clear on that point, the rest falls in place nicely.

Stick to your guns. Explain that you have all of the physical evidence you need, and are ready to go to court and hire an attorney. You will immediately notice that this is the last thing the insurance adjuster wants you to do.

As in any other negotiation, the first offer is almost always not the best offer. Like a good poker player, the adjuster will not show his or her had immediately. For the same reason, your first settlement demand cannot be a drop dead, take it or leave position. You should expect to bargain downwards from your initial position, and make the initial offer high enough to permit this.

Be ready and willing to break off negotiations. The insurance adjuster in under pressure to close files, and is evaluated on his success in doing so. There is motivation on his part to resolve the matter, and this creates leverage. The more you can convince the adjuster that you are willing to go the long haul and take your chances in court, the better.

When you attempt to settle a claim timing can also be important. For example, the worst possible time to negotiate is in December. This is because the insurance companies are flooded with calls from people with pending claims, hoping to settle in time for Christmas. This makes response times much slower. Even worse, sensing panic on the other side, the adjusters tend to reduce their offers to take advantage of the situation. Scrooge would be proud.

There are serious problems during the summer vacation period. At any given time, half the people needed to resolve a claim within the company are out of town. This goes not only for adjusters, but also the upper level supervisors who have authority to significantly raise an offer.

On the other hand, it can be to your advantage to negotiation in the periods following these times. The two weeks following Christmas are the best time of the year to attempt to settle a case. Many companies have year-end evaluations, and for various reasons, need to get liabilities off the books. The adjuster might spend a little more on your claim to make his or her numbers look better at the right time.

This is a long shot, but it can be a huge advantage to deal with an adjuster who is leaving the company. If you get this opportunity, push to resolve things before the file is transferred. They will not have the authority to simply give you whatever you want, but most likely will much less interested in protecting their "reserves" (in other words, spending less on the settlement than the company authorized them to.)

If you are able to get an acceptable offer, ask for a timetable as to when you might receive the settlement package. Ten days to two weeks would be a typical response. Often, particularly where an attorney is not involved, the adjuster will send only the release, and forward the check after receiving the signed release documents.

It is also worth knowing that the check is invariably sent in a plain envelope, so it is easily confused with junk mail. If you are expecting a settlement check, make sure that you open your mail carefully, and that your family members are aware of the situation.

CHAPTER FIVE: TRIAL.

If you have to file suit, you need a lawyer. Plain and simple, the courtroom is no place for untrained amateurs. The litigation process is complicated, and an experienced trail lawyer can carve up a non-attorney pretty much effortlessly.

This is not meant as an insult. I do not mean to imply that attorneys are smarter than other people, or superior. Simply put, an individual who specializes in a trade will almost always outperform a person who does not. I like to think of myself as a fairly intelligent person, but if the need arises, I will hire a surgeon to remove my appendix.

The defense attorney who already has your file spends most of his life litigating cases much like yours. He has already made all the mistakes, and learned what does and does not work. He has most likely studied the jury panel, and knows all the local judges. He is well paid to do this by a multinational corporation with all sorts of options. In other words, he is good.

At this point, you need to hand the case over to an equally good profession. The only exception to this would be a minor case that would be handled in small claims court, where the rules are written to accommodate non-attorneys.

Of course, there is the possibility that you are having trouble getting a lawyer. If you've shopped your case all over town with no luck, this is not a good sign. Solid personal injury cases do not grow on trees, and lawyers fight for their share of this market. The fact that you are getting the cold shoulder in all probability means that your case is not as strong as you believe it to be.

As a last resort, try your state bar lawyer referral agency. This is a referral service operated by your state judiciary, which will refer you to an attorney who practices in the area of law in which you have a need. The benefit of this is that you will probably get someone who does not know you, is unfamiliar with your situation, and without preconceived notions.

It is essential that you know about deadlines. There is a statute of limitations which applies to a lawsuit of this kind. Before that date has passed, the lawsuit must be filed in the courthouse and served on the defendant. If all of this has not been done, there can be no recovery.

In many states, the injured party has the right to file suit for a period of three years following the date of the accident. However, and this is crucial, many states have a two year statute of limitations. The point is that you need to find out immediately how long you have to file your case, and be mindful of the time limit.

There is also a trend towards alternate dispute resolution. This would primarily include mediation and arbitration. Of the two, mediation is the less difficult and problematic for a non- attorney, as it can only resolve a case by the agreement of the parties. In a nutshell, a mediator is a person who hears arguments presented by either side in a case. He then attempts to help the opposing sides find common ground and settle. If this is unsuccessful, the mediator declares an "impasse" and the case is scheduled for trial.

An arbitrator, by contrast, acts as a kind of a judge. In arbitration evidence will be presented in much the same manner as in a trial. However, the process is unusually less formal in an attempt to make the process faster and less expensive. The arbitrator will make findings of fact, and will in fact decide the case. If either party is unhappy with the result of arbitration, he or she generally has the right to request a trial by jury.

If you are required to participate in either of these, know that there will be a separate set of rules for the process, independent and unique from the court rules. The mediator or arbitrator will probably send you a copy of these rules prior to your hearing.

Unfortunately, you might also have to pay the mediator or arbitrator out of your own pocket. Some jurisdictions refer these duties to court staff, and do not charge additional fees. However, in many more, the process will cost you hundreds of dollars and a great deal of time.

It is most important to keep in mind that neither can force you to settle your case. If you are unhappy with the result of mediation, simply refuse the last offer and go home. If your arbitration hearing ends unfavorably, follow the procedure and request a trial by jury.

Again, I highly recommend against representing yourself in a lawsuit beyond the small claims court level. In addition to the reasons we have already discussed, there is the fact that court rosters are highly unpredictable. A case filed by a non-attorney can be called for trial very quickly, due to, among other things, the orchestrations of defense counsel.

It is not possible in the context of a book to teach all of the skills necessary to competently try a personal injury case. It is not even possible to catalogue all of the ways that opposing counsel can get a case thrown out of court on a technicality. Simply put, if your case remains unresolved past the mediation/arbitration stage, do what it takes to get the help you need. If it has the potential to generate a reasonable fee, somebody will be willing to get involved. If not, you should seriously consider whether it should be going forward in the first place.

If all else fails and you will be trying your case on a *pro se* basis, contact your neighborhood legal assistance program, your state bar, or visit an area law library. Ask for the rules of civil procedure for the jurisdiction in which the case will be heard, and carefully review all applicable rules.

You should also search for what are called "secondary sources." These would be books and other materials intended to teach the skills necessary to present your case. The state bar division for continuing legal education should have materials which will help in this regard. If you must make the ill-advised decision to go it alone, study as much material of this sort as possible before you ever file a lawsuit.

The good news is that the things needed to prove your case should already be at hand, provided you followed the advice given earlier in this book. You will already have contact information for important witnesses, photographs and video evidence from the scene of the accident, and complete medical documentation. These are the things that get the attention of a jury. They might well be persuasive in spite of any lack of polish in your presentation.

CONCLUSION:

It has been estimated that ninety five percent of personal injury cases settle out of court. If you are not found at fault, or partially at fault, the chances of your reaching a settlement are good.

The better prepared you are to present your case to a judge, jury, or other fact finder, the better the chance that you will not have to. By taking the steps outlined in this book, you can document and increase the value of your claim, and avoid the kind of catastrophic errors which could alternately ruin it.

If you are not represented by an attorney, the insurance adjuster will most likely negotiate with you based on the medical records. This means you will not need to write a demand letter. However, if you choose to do so, be sure to explain why the insured party is liable to you, the extent of your damages and to what you are entitled. Always be sure to include your date of loss, the claim number, and the names of all parties involved in the accident. Keep a copy of anything sent to the insurance company, especially medical records, photographs, or other evidence.

While in negotiation with the adjuster, be aware of the statute of limitations for your case. The insurance company will not advise you if your time to file is running out. Instead, they will mark their calendar and count the days.

If it becomes necessary to file suit, attempt to do so at least ninety days before the case would be statutorily barred. The process is complicated and you may need more time than you expect.

Best wishes and good luck!

Robert Rushing, Jr.

Robert5286@aol.com

www.ingramcontent.com/pod-product-compliance
Lightning Source LLC
Chambersburg PA
CBHW070723180526
45167CB00004B/1586